D0975472

ANCIENT ANIMALS

PLESIOSAUR

Sarah L. Thomson

Illustrated by **Andrew Plant**

Charlesbridge

To the teachers at Longfellow Elementary School—S. L. T.

For all the fossil hunters of Kronosaurus Korner, discovering Australia's own prehistoric inland sea—A. P.

The plesiosaur (PLEE-see-oh-sore) featured in the beginning of this book is *Elasmosaurus platyurus*.

Special thanks to Carl Mehling at the American Museum of Natural History for his expertise.

Published by Charlesbridge
85 Main Street
Watertown, MA 02472
(617) 926-0329
www.charlesbridge.com

Library of Congress Cataloging-in-Publication Data
Names: Thomson, Sarah L., author. | Plant, Andrew, illustrator.
Title: Ancient animals. Plesiosaur / Sarah L. Thomson; illustrated by Andrew Plant.
Other titles: Plesiosaur
Description: Watertown, MA: Charlesbridge, [2017]
Identifiers: LCCN 2016009217 (print) | LCCN 2016010589 (ebook) | ISBN 9781580895422 (reinforced for library use) | ISBN 9781607348641 (ebook) | ISBN 9781607348658 (ebook pdf)
Subjects: LCSH: Plesiosaurus—Juvenile literature. | Marine reptiles, Fossil—Juvenile literature.
Classification: LCC QE862.P4 T46 2017 (print) | LCC QE862.P4 (ebook) | DDC 567.9/37—dc23
LC record available at http://lccn.loc.gov/2016009217

Protosphyraena

Printed in China
(hc) 10 9 8 7 6 5 4 3 2 1

Illustrations done in acrylic gouache on acid-free cartridge paper
Display type set in Mindcrime AOE by Astigmatic
Text type set in Janson Text by Linotype
Color separations by JCP Studios, Cremorne, Victoria, Australia
Printed by 1010 Printing International Limited in Huizhou, Guangdong, China
Production supervision by Brian G. Walker
Designed by Martha MacLeod Sikkema

This is Kansas
ninety million years ago.
A warm, shallow sea
covered the land.

Something that looked small
swam up from the bottom.
It swam past a squid.
It swam past a turtle
with a shell as large
as the hood of a car.
It swam toward
a school of fish.

Protostega

The swimmer
did not seem
to be an enemy.
It was not a big hunter
like a shark
or a mosasaur.
So the fish kept eating.

young *Tusoteuthis*

Enchodus

Enchodus

young *Tusoteuthis*

The swimmer got closer.
A small head
on a long neck
darted at a fish.
It grabbed the fish
with sharp, thin teeth.
It gulped the meal down
in one bite.

Enchodus

The hunter was a plesiosaur.
Its neck was three times as long
as a giraffe's.
Its huge body was hidden
in the dark water.
A pile of smooth stones
sat in its stomach.
The stones may have
helped to crush food.

Plesiosaurs lived on earth
for about 150 million years.
There were many kinds.
Some had long necks.
Some had short ones.
Some plesiosaurs were
only a bit longer
than a broomstick.
Some could have stretched
halfway across
a basketball court.

Kronosaurus
Dolichorhynchops
Styxosaurus
Nichollssaura

Plesiosaurs were reptiles.
Other reptiles lived
at the same time.
Crocodiles and turtles
and mosasaurs
swam in the sea.
Pterosaurs flew
through the air.
Dinosaurs walked
on the land.

Pteranodon
Clidastes (mosasaur)
Terminonaris
Toxochelys

Some reptiles had scales.
Some had smooth skin.
Some had feathers.
Some were covered in fuzz.
None could breathe underwater
as fish do.
None fed milk to their babies
as mammals do.

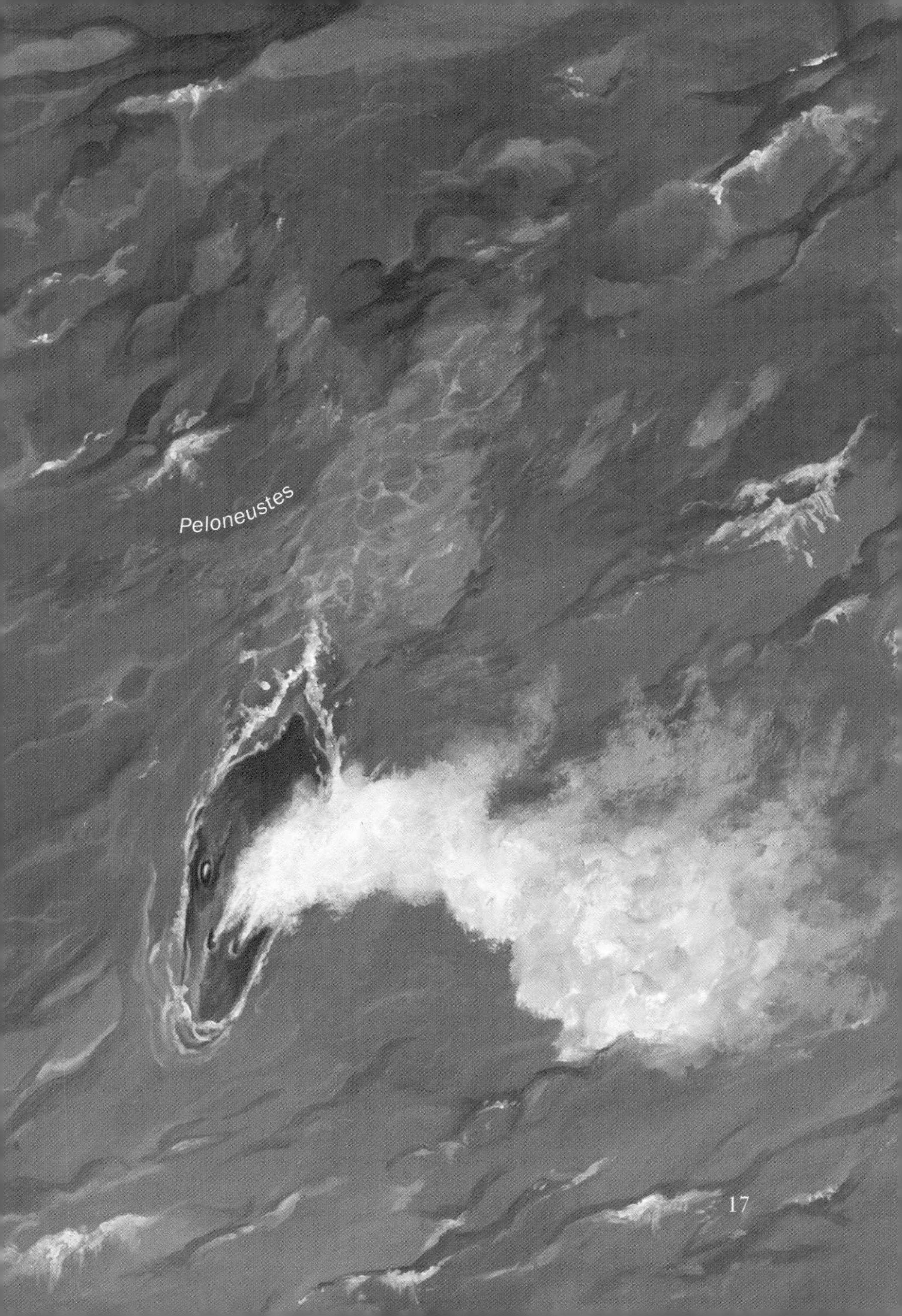
Peloneustes

Flying reptiles had wings.
Reptiles that lived on land
had legs and feet.
Reptiles in the sea
had flippers and fins.
A plesiosaur had four flippers.
Maybe it paddled
like a duck.
Maybe it glided
like a sea turtle.

Kronosaurus

Most reptiles on land
lay eggs.
But if ocean reptiles
lay eggs underwater,
the babies inside
will drown.
Plesiosaurs could not
lay eggs in the sea.
And they could not crawl
onto the land
to make nests.
They gave birth
to their babies.

Nichollsaura

Most reptile babies
do not need parents.
But a few reptile parents
look after their young.
Crocodiles guard their hatchlings.
A dinosaur called *Oviraptor*
sat on its nest.
Maybe plesiosaur parents
also kept their babies safe
from hungry hunters.
We are not sure.
One day we may find out.

Cretoxyrhina

Life became harder for plesiosaurs
about eighty-five million years ago.
There were new animals
in the ocean.
Quick-swimming fish
and deadly mosasaurs
hunted plesiosaurs
and their prey.

Tylosaurus (mosasaur)
Dolichorhynchops (plesiosaur)

And then sixty-five million years ago,
there were new problems.
The weather grew warmer.
Many volcanoes erupted.
And a rock from space
crashed into Earth.
This caused floods and fires.
Clouds of dust and ash
hid the sun.
Few plants could grow.
Many animals starved.

After that time
there were no more plesiosaurs.
No more mosasaurs.
No more giant dinosaurs.
They all became extinct.
But we can find fossils
of their bones today.
We can learn about the days
when large reptiles
roamed the land and the air
and the sea.

Most reptiles spend
their lives on land.
The ones that live in the sea
are called marine reptiles.
Some have become extinct.
Others are alive today.

Ichthyosaur

- Up to 50 feet long
- Extinct about 95 million years ago
- Looked a lot like today's fast-swimming fish and dolphins

Mosasaur

- Up to 50 feet long
- Extinct 65 million years ago
- A predatory reptile with a shape like a snake or eel

Leatherback sea turtle
- Up to 7 feet long
- Atlantic, Pacific, and Indian Oceans and the Mediterranean Sea
- Biggest sea turtle alive today

Marine iguana
- Up to 5 feet long
- Galápagos Islands
- Only lizard that spends much of its life in the water

Saltwater crocodile
- Up to 20 feet long
- Southeast Asia and Australia
- Biggest crocodile alive today

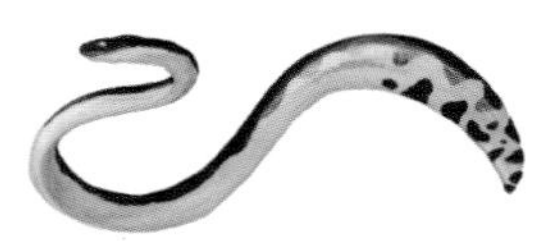

Sea snake
- Up to 8 feet long
- Indian and Pacific Oceans
- A venomous snake with a flattened tail for swimming

More to Discover

Do you want to find out more about plesiosaurs and other extinct marine reptiles? These books, videos, and websites are good places to start.

Books

Arnold, Caroline. *Giant Sea Reptiles of the Dinosaur Age*. New York: Clarion Books, 2007.

Collard, Sneed B. III. *Reign of the Sea Dragons.* Watertown, MA: Charlesbridge, 2008.

Loxton, Daniel. *Tales of Prehistoric Life: Plesiosaur Peril.* Toronto: Kids Can Press, 2014.

Videos

"T-Rex of the Deep." *Monsters Resurrected.* Season 1. Episode 2. Discovery Channel, 2009.

"Fight for Life." *Planet Dinosaur.* Season 1. Episode 4. BBC America, 2011.

Websites

See pictures of plesiosaurs and fossils.
www.oceansofkansas.com/plesiosaur.html

Discover details about how plesiosaurs lived.
www.bbc.co.uk/nature/life/Plesiosaur

The first plesiosaur fossil was discovered by Mary Anning in England in 1823. You can read about her life and watch a video.
www.bbc.co.uk/schools/primaryhistory/famouspeople/mary_anning
Or you can enter "Mary Anning" into your favorite search engine to find out more.